Ela Area
275 Mohawk Trail, Lake Zurich, IL 60047
(847) 438-3433
www.eapl.org

31241008801279

DISCARDED

COMPUTER PIONEERS

Mark Zuckerberg

Founder of Facebook

Katie Kawa

PowerKiDS press.

New York

Published in 2017 by The Rosen Publishing Group, Inc.
29 East 21st Street, New York, NY 10010

Copyright © 2017 by The Rosen Publishing Group, Inc.

All rights reserved. No part of this book may be reproduced in any form without permission in writing from the publisher, except by a reviewer.

First Edition

Editor: Caitlin McAneney
Book Design: Mickey Harmon

Photo Credits: Cover, pp. 1, 3–24, 26–32 (background) yxowert/Shutterstock.com; cover (Mark Zuckerberg), p. 9 (main) Frederic Legrand - COMEO/Shutterstock.com; p. 5 Kobby Dagan/Shutterstock.com; pp. 7, 29 catwalker/Shutterstock.com; p. 9 (screen) Annette Shaff/Shutterstock.com; p. 11 Art Phaneuf Photography/Shutterstock.com; p. 13 C Flanigan/Contributor/FilmMagic/Getty Images; p. 15 Boston Globe/Contributor/Getty Images; p. 17 Blend Images/Shutterstock.com; p. 19 Justin Sullivan/Staff/Getty Images News/Getty Images; pp. 21, 27 Bloomberg/Contributor/Getty Images; p. 23 (Zuckerberg) AFP/Stringer/Getty Images; p. 23 (Sandberg) Chip Somodevilla/Staff/Getty Images News/Getty Images; p. 25 Stephen Lovekin/Staff/Getty Images Entertainment/Getty Images.

Library of Congress Cataloging-in-Publication Data

Kawa, Katie, author.
 Mark Zuckerberg : founder of facebook / Katie Kawa.
    pages cm. — (Computer pioneers)
 Includes index.
ISBN 978-1-5081-4838-8 (pbk.)
ISBN 978-1-5081-4770-1 (6 pack)
ISBN 978-1-5081-4803-6 (library binding)
1. Zuckerberg, Mark, 1984—Juvenile literature. 2. Facebook (Firm)—Juvenile literature. 3. Facebook (Electronic resource)—Juvenile literature. 4. Online social networks—Juvenile literature. 5. Webmasters—United States—Biography—Juvenile literature. I. Title.
HM743.F33K39 2017
006.7'54092—dc23
[B]
                                    2015031616

Manufactured in the United States of America

CPSIA Compliance Information: Batch #BS16PK: For Further Information contact Rosen Publishing, New York, New York at 1-800-237-9932

Contents

The Face of Facebook

Mark Zuckerberg is the founder, chairman, and **chief executive officer** (CEO) of one of the most influential social media platforms in the world: Facebook. However, he didn't start out with the dream of being the most famous computer programmer of his generation. Growing up, he was just a kid who loved computers and wanted to use them to have fun with his friends and family.

The relationship between computers and friendships has been at the heart of Facebook since Zuckerberg created it with friends in his Harvard dorm room. What started as a program created to develop and strengthen social networks at Harvard soon grew into something that connects people around the world. This was all because Zuckerberg wanted to use his computer skills to bring people together.

Mark Zuckerberg is the youngest self-made billionaire to ever appear on *Forbes* magazine's list of billionaires. He was able to turn his love for computers into a very successful career!

facebook

I facebook

Learning from Dad

Mark Zuckerberg was born on May 14, 1984, and raised in Dobbs Ferry, New York. His parents were both successful; his father, Edward, is a dentist, and his mother, Karen, is a **psychiatrist**. After having children, Karen stopped practicing psychiatry for a while, but she continued to work as her husband's office manager. Karen and Edward also have three daughters: Arielle, Randi, and Donna.

Edward introduced his son to computers at a young age. In fact, he was the first person to teach Zuckerberg computer programming! He showed his son how to work with the BASIC programming language. Because Edward's dental office was connected to their home, young Zuckerberg had access to a lot of computers to work with and study as his interest in programming grew.

Zuckerberg's father introduced him to the exciting world of computer programming at a young age, and he never looked back!

Early Computing

Computer programming has interested Zuckerberg since he was young. What exactly is computer programming? It's the creation of different sets of instructions that allow computers to do certain tasks. People turn information into a language computers understand through a process called coding. There are many different **programming languages** used to tell computers what to do. Some of these are C++, Java, and Ruby. Young people today can take classes, read books, or visit websites that can teach them how to code.

ZuckNet and Beyond

After he learned programming from his father, Zuckerberg's parents hired a computer tutor to teach him even more. Then, he started taking advanced computer classes at a college near his home. While other kids were buying computer games in middle school, Zuckerberg was busy creating them! His friends would come over to his house, and Zuckerberg would use his coding skills to create new computer games for them to play.

Zuckerberg soon began using his skills at home and around his father's office. When his father wanted to find a better communication system for his office, Zuckerberg stepped in to help. At only 12 years old, he programmed the computers around the house and office to send messages to one another. Zuckerberg called this messaging system ZuckNet.

Long before Zuckerberg helped develop Facebook's instant messaging system, he created an early form of instant messaging with ZuckNet.

Excelling at Exeter

Zuckerberg attended a local high school, but he later transferred to Phillips Exeter Academy, which is a private boarding school in New Hampshire. At this school—often just called Exeter—Zuckerberg continued to sharpen his math, science, and coding skills.

For Zuckerberg's final project at Exeter, he worked with a friend named Adam D'Angelo to create software, or a set of programs, called Synapse. This software worked by using **artificial intelligence**. It would monitor all the songs played on a person's computer and make playlists based on what that person liked to listen to.

Zuckerberg graduated from Phillips Exeter Academy, shown here, in 2002.

Word soon got out about Synapse. Major companies such as Microsoft offered to pay D'Angelo and Zuckerberg a lot of money to come work for them. However, both young men chose to go to college instead.

From CourseMatch to The Facebook

Zuckerberg chose not to sell Synapse and start working right after high school because he wanted to attend Harvard University in Massachusetts. In 2002, Zuckerberg started his education at Harvard, where he studied computer science.

During Zuckerberg's time at Harvard, he became known for creating computer programs that were very popular with his fellow students. One popular program was called CourseMatch. This program helped Harvard students choose their classes by allowing them to see what classes their fellow students were taking.

The early programs Zuckerberg developed at Harvard were based on the idea of connecting people through the Internet. That idea was the central focus for a website Zuckerberg and two roommates—Dustin Moskovitz and Chris Hughes—launched in February 2004: The Facebook.

Zuckerberg's future was shaped by his time at Harvard in more ways than one. While he was there, he also met his wife, Priscilla Chan. They were married on May 19, 2012.

Legal Battles

Not everyone at Harvard was excited about The Facebook. Three students—Divya Narendra and twins Cameron and Tyler Winklevoss—believed Zuckerberg got the idea for his website from a project he'd originally agreed to work on for them, which was called Harvard Connection. The three men sued Zuckerberg, but a **settlement** was eventually reached. Zuckerberg also faced a legal battle with one of his original Facebook co-founders, Eduardo Saverin. Saverin sued Zuckerberg after his role in the company was greatly reduced, but a settlement was also reached in that lawsuit.

Starting Small

The Facebook, which was renamed Facebook in 2005, started as a way for Harvard students to connect with one another. Zuckerberg and his friends created software that allowed people with a Harvard email address to create their own Facebook page to be seen by other Harvard students. This page included a photo and basic information, such as their name, birthday, and email address.

Facebook started small. It was created in a dorm room by a group of young men who loved to code for fun. It started with only one server. A server is the main computer in a network that provides services to others in the network, such as Facebook users. This single server cost $85 a month to run. Now, Facebook needs tens of thousands of servers in each of its **data centers**.

Shown here is Kirkland House at Harvard, which is where Zuckerberg lived when he created Facebook. The name "Facebook" came from lists of students given out at Harvard and other schools to help those students get to know each other better.

Conserving with Servers

Servers use a lot of energy, so Facebook is working to make sure its data centers are as environmentally friendly as possible. One of its data centers is located in Luleå, Sweden. This location was chosen in part because it's naturally cold enough to keep the servers from overheating. This conserves energy that would have otherwise been spent on air conditioning to keep the servers in a cool environment. It also conserves water, which is used in cooling systems for servers.

The "Social Graph"

When Zuckerberg first created Facebook, it was one of a number of early social networking websites. However, it was different because of its focus on creating and developing trusted relationships. Students who joined Facebook used their real name and email address. This allowed them to connect with their friends—and friends of friends—through the Internet. Zuckerberg often calls this network of trusted relationships at the center of Facebook the "social graph."

Less than a month after Facebook was created and became the talk of Harvard, it expanded to other schools. Yale University in Connecticut, Columbia University in New York, and Stanford University in California all had access to Facebook by March 2004.

Zuckerberg created Facebook as a way for college students to connect with their classmates. However, Facebook is now geared toward the social graphs of people of all ages and backgrounds.

In the first month, around 7,500 users joined Facebook. Students spread the word about Facebook to their friends, and the website's popularity continued to grow.

Growing Quickly

In June 2004, Zuckerberg and his co-founders moved to Palo Alto, California, to focus on getting more money for Facebook's development. As Facebook continued to grow, Zuckerberg left Harvard to focus on running the company and creating new software for it. Less than a year after its creation, Facebook reached over 1 million active users.

By April 2005, Facebook was believed to be worth $100 million. This was a huge difference from the $85 a month it cost Zuckerberg to run the website when it first started! Later in 2005, Facebook was opened to high school students, and students in foreign countries were beginning to join the website, too. Over 6 million people were using Facebook by the end of that year.

In 2011, President Barack Obama met with Mark Zuckerberg at Facebook's offices in Palo Alto, California. California is the home of most major Internet companies. Mark decided to move there in 2004.

News Feed Changes Everything

For the first two years of Facebook's existence, people needed to click on individual profiles to find out what was going on in their friends' lives. All that changed, however, on September 5, 2006. That was when Facebook **launched** a new feature called News Feed.

News Feed was unlike anything anyone had ever seen on the Internet before. It took all the latest information and changes from the profiles of a user's friends and put them in one place for that user to easily see. News Feed changed the way people found out information about their friends' lives. It inspired the format of many social media platforms that came later, such as Twitter and Instagram. Because of Facebook, our social lives—both online and away from our computers—will never be the same.

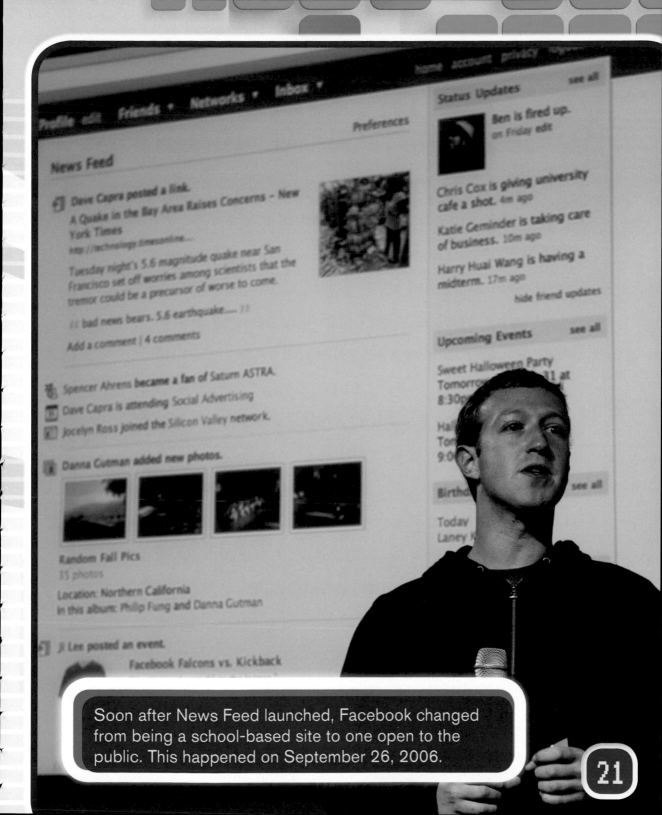

Soon after News Feed launched, Facebook changed from being a school-based site to one open to the public. This happened on September 26, 2006.

21

Continuing to Connect

As of June 2015, Facebook had 10,955 employees. There are many things that might attract people to a job at Facebook, such as free food and video games to play in a recreation center. However, working for Mark Zuckerberg may be one of the best things about working there. His belief in using the Internet to connect people has connected him with some of the brightest engineers and computer programmers in the world.

Zuckerberg is always looking for new ways to use computers to allow people to share what matters to them. That's why he announced in April 2012 that Facebook was acquiring Instagram, a popular photo-sharing platform. Zuckerberg knew Instagram was a great way for Facebook's users to share photos with one another.

The social graph is the driving force behind everything Mark does at Facebook, including the **acquisition** of Instagram.

Sheryl Sandberg

Zuckerberg continues to lead Facebook into the future as its CEO, but its chief operating officer (COO) is Sheryl Sandberg. It's Sheryl's job to manage the business operation of Facebook. Sheryl graduated from Harvard Business School and has held many important jobs—including work at the World Bank in Washington, D.C.—before joining Facebook as COO in 2008. Sheryl's business sense has been a huge factor in Facebook's growth since 2008. She's also the founder of Lean In, an organization dedicated to helping women achieve their career goals.

A Computer Celebrity

Today, Zuckerberg's no longer just a kid with a computer and a dream of connecting people. He's a celebrity known around the world for his contributions to social media technology. In 2010, *Time* magazine named Zuckerberg its Person of the Year.

That same year, a major movie about the creation of Facebook was released. *The Social Network* won three Academy Awards, which are awards given for the highest achievements in film each year.

As Zuckerberg's **status** as a celebrity has continued to rise, so has Facebook's influence around the world. In June 2015, Facebook reported that an average of 968 million people use the website every day! Over 80 percent of those users are from countries other than the United States and Canada.

Mark actually went to see *The Social Network* with a group of Facebook employees. He said afterward that the movie presented a lot of false information about him and his reasons for creating Facebook. This is Jesse Eisenberg, who played Zuckerberg in the movie.

Helping Others

In recent years, Zuckerberg has become known for much more than just his coding skills and "social graph" vision. He's also famous for his philanthropy, or his support of charitable causes. In fact, on December 9, 2010, Zuckerberg pledged to **donate** at least half his wealth to charity over his lifetime.

Zuckerberg is also a big supporter of children's education. In 2010, he donated $100 million to the Newark, New Jersey, school system, even though he never lived in Newark himself. In 2012, Zuckerberg and his wife donated nearly $500 million to the Silicon Valley Community Foundation. This foundation is known for supporting a variety of causes, including education for **immigrants** and help for people affected by wildfires in California.

Zuckerberg and his wife, Priscilla Chan, announced the birth of their daughter Max in December 2015. Zuckerberg also announced that he'd donate around $45 billion to charitable causes during his lifetime as part of the Chan Zuckerberg Initiative. He and his wife want to make the world a better place for their daughter and people everywhere.

Leading a New Age

Mark Zuckerberg has spent most of his life finding ways for computers to bring people closer to their friends and family. Whether he was programming computer games for his friends or developing the latest technology for Facebook, Zuckerberg has always been dedicated to keeping the social graph at the heart of everything he does.

With the creation of Facebook, Zuckerberg forever changed the way we interact with people in our social networks. Millions of people of all ages from all over the world are interacting with family and friends on Facebook right now. They wouldn't be doing that without the vision and skills of Mark Zuckerberg. He's one of the leaders of this new age of social media—changing the world one Facebook update at a time.

Zuckerberg's belief that computers can strengthen social relationships has changed the world!

Timeline

May 14, 1984
Zuckerberg is born near Dobbs Ferry, New York.

1996
Zuckerberg creates the ZuckNet instant messaging system.

2002
Zuckerberg graduates from Phillips Exeter Academy and begins his studies at Harvard University.

February 2004
Zuckerberg and his roommates launch The Facebook, which is later renamed Facebook.

March 2004
Facebook expands to Yale, Columbia, and Stanford.

June 2004
Zuckerberg moves to Palo Alto, California, with the other creators of Facebook.

December 2004
Facebook reaches 1 million users.

2005
Facebook opens to high school students.

September 2006
Facebook launches News Feed and opens to the public.

2010
Zuckerberg is named *Time* magazine's Person of the Year. He is also the subject of the movie *The Social Network*.

December 9, 2010
Zuckerberg pledges to donate at least half his wealth to charity during his lifetime.

April 2012
Zuckerberg announces that Facebook has acquired Instagram.

May 19, 2012
Zuckerberg marries Priscilla Chan.

Glossary

acquisition: The act of getting something.

artificial intelligence: An area of computer science that deals with giving machines the ability to seem like they have human intelligence.

chief executive officer: The person who has the most authority in an organization or business.

data center: A place that houses a large group of computer servers typically used by organizations for storing, processing, and distributing large amounts of data.

donate: To give something in order to help a person or organization.

immigrant: A person who comes to a country to live there.

launch: To officially start something.

programming language: A formal language designed to communicate instructions to a machine, especially a computer.

psychiatrist: A person who practices a branch of medicine that deals with mental or emotional disorders.

settlement: A formal agreement that ends an argument or dispute.

status: The rank of someone compared to others in a society.

Index

Websites

Due to the changing nature of Internet links, PowerKids Press has developed an online list of websites related to the subject of this book. This site is updated regularly. Please use this link to access the list: www.powerkidslinks.com/compio/zucke